Unprecedented Press

The Best Kids Explore Montana © 2024 by Joshua Best

All rights reserved. No part of this publication may be reproduced, distributed, or transmitted in any form or by any means, including photocopying, recording, or other electronic or mechanical methods, without the prior written permission of the publisher or author, except in the case of brief quotations embodied in critical reviews and certain other noncommercial uses permitted by copyright law. For permission requests, email the publisher or author at addresses below:

Contact the publisher:
Unprecedented Press LLC - 229 W Main Ave, Zeeland, MI 49464
www.unprecedentedpress.com | info@unprecedentedpress.com
instagram: unprecedentedpress

ISBN: 979-8-9867126-2-8

Ingram Printing & Distribution, 2024

First Edition

the BEST KIDS explore

FEATURING: maps, reviews, travel tips, and true tales of family adventures

MONTANA
& NORTH DAKOTA

An illustrated, story-driven travel guide for kids

CONTENTS

MEET THE KIDS 4

LODGING & TRANSPORT 6

STORIES:

TEDDY'S WAY 8
in Dickinson, ND

THE BRIDGE 16
in Bozeman, MT

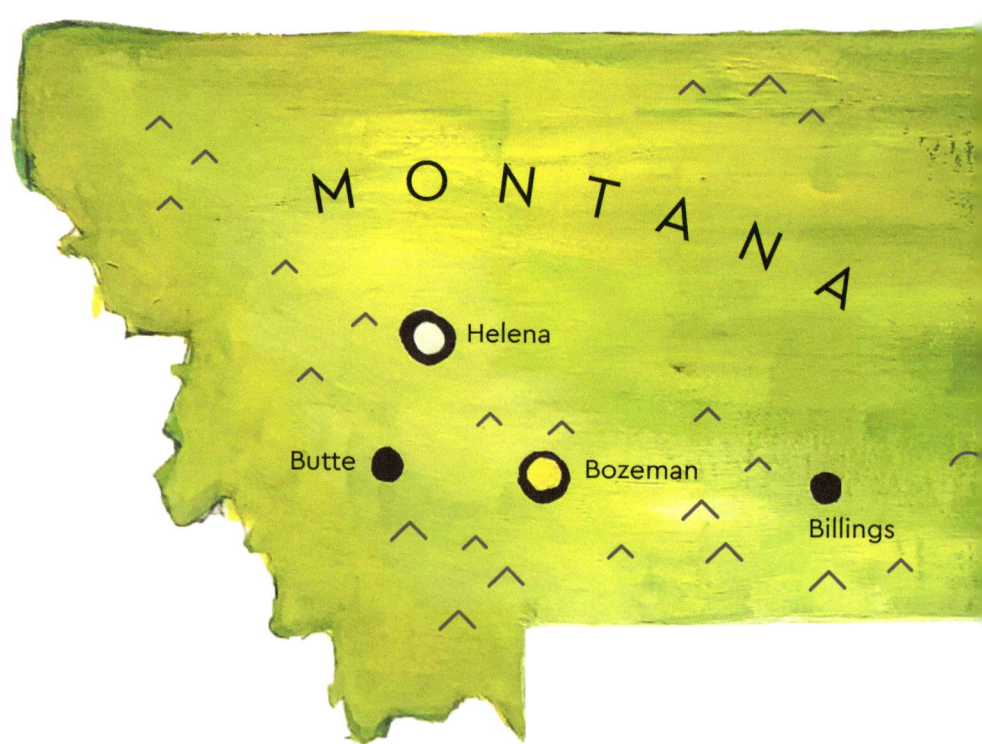

HERDS & TURDS 22
in Bozeman, MT

FAR FROM PLAIN 28
in Fargo, ND

LITTLE DETAILS 34
BEST BITES 35
BEST BETS 36
BUMPS IN THE ROAD 38

MEET THE KIDS

Exploring is the best. Exploring lets you discover the cool things around you – things you didn't know were there before. That's what makes it so much fun! It's exciting to find out what's around the corner, across the border and beyond the horizon.

The Best kids are explorers. They love finding new places to play and discovering new ways to have fun. The oldest is Frederick – he has orange hair. The middle child is Edith – she has brown hair. The youngest is Hugo – he has yellow hair. The Best kids are half American and half Canadian. They live in Michigan.

In this book, the kids travel to the states of North Dakota and Montana. At the time of their expedition, Frederick was seven years old, Edith was six years old, and Hugo was two years old. This trip occurred in the month of July.

LODGING & TRANSPORT

The Best family travelled to Montana and North Dakota by car. They all piled into their grey Chevy Traverse and hit the road. Instead of taking the southern route through Chicago, they went north across Michigan's Upper Peninsula. On this trip, they were trying hard to avoid crowds because of COVID-19. They tackled the journey to Bozeman, Montana with three days of driving, spending one night in Wisconsin, and one in North Dakota.

TOWNPLACE SUITES

👦 ★★
👧 ★★★½
👦 ★★★

For lodging, the kids stayed three nights at Townplace Suites in Dickinson, North Dakota. The hotel was just a short drive away from Theodore Roosevelt National Park.

The kids found the hotel to be clean and comfortable, but it was over-crowded and the breakfast was made up of only packaged goods as a COVID safety precaution.

Their favorite place to stay was at their Uncle Kevin and Aunt Carolynn's house in Bozeman, Montana.

TEDDY'S WAY

The year was 2020. Along with the rest of the world, the Best kids were trapped at home because of the global pandemic. They couldn't go to school and classes were virtual. They couldn't even see their friends unless they were socially distant. They understood why it was important, and they wanted to protect their neighbors, 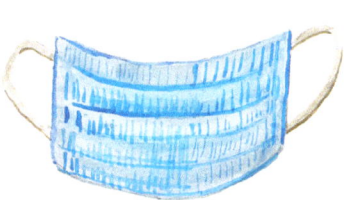 but for a bunch of expolorers, staying at home for a long period of time can be tough!

As the Bests approached the fifth month of limited mobility, they decided it was finally safe to venture out, so they plotted a rural road trip and headed out west. With fewer services available for travelers and extra precautions taken (masks, sanitizer, and a big red cooler full of snacks), they truly felt like old fashioned explorers who were off the grid. Despite the challenges in front of them, they were certain that a dose of adventure would help them recover from this difficult time.

To avoid large crowds, they packed up their Chevy Traverse, and drove through Michigan's Upper Peninsula (instead of through Chicago). It was a longer route around Lake Michigan, but it was a beautiful drive.

On their journey, they rested briefly in Wisconsin, and then Minnesota, before arriving in the town of Dickinson, North Dakota. It was dark out when they arrived at TownePlace Suites, which was their base for exploring Theodore Roosevelt National Park. Each of

the kids
woke up
from sleeping in
the car, put on their
backpacks and grabbed
their pillows (another COVID
precaution). To avoid elevators, they
lugged their belongings up four flights of
stairs to reach their room.

Knowing the hotel would only be offering prepackaged, processed breakfast, the kids' mom came prepared. Before they left on their western journey, she filled their red, metal cooler with fresh food for the family. This came in handy on their first morning in the hotel as they recovered from their long drive.

With bananas and Lärabars in hand, the Best kids filed into the car at 8:30 in the morning. They were headed to the northern unit of Theodore Roosevelt National Park.

As they drove north along the county road, they passed by rolling hills of green grass, and fields filled with

farm animals. Eventually, they approached the gates of the national park where the landscape became more rocky, with exposed cliffs and unique rock formations. The ranger at the entry booth offered them each a junior ranger badge and a workbook with activities. The kids were excited about this unexpected gift!

After stopping to examine the map and their options, they entered the park.

"Keep your eyes peeled!" Their dad urged.

"There's wildlife around here!" Said their mom.

With the windows rolled down, Frederick, Edith and Hugo scoured the landscape for signs of life like the kids from Jurassic Park.

"What's that?!" Yelled Frederick.

The car came to a stop and they jumped out.

"That's Bison dung." Explained their dad. Hugo still looked confused.

"Poop from a buffalo." Dad added. Hugo gasped.

The main destination on this route was Riverbend Overlook. On the way there, they spotted wild longhorn cattle, and after they parked, Edith saw a deer on the foot path.

As they continued on their way to the overlook, they spotted a structure made of log and stone that marked the stomping ground of Theodore Roosevelt, President of the United States in the early 1900s. At the park, the kids learned that he traveled to North Dakota in search of peace and comfort after his wife and mother died (in the same week) in New York City.

As the Best family looked out over the ridge, they understood how the landscape could salve a weary soul. They had also been through a difficult season: virtual school, mask mandates and lockdowns. The view from the River Bend Overlook was incredible; they could see the entire valley. They took it all in and quietly reaffirmed their commitment to continue adventuring despite adversity. As they walked back up the trail, the kids' mom and dad wiped tears from their eyes and gave each of the kids a big hug.

THE BRIDGE

Like most families, the Bests endured challenging situations because of the pandemic. Not only were they unable to visit their grandparents and cousins in Canada for nearly two years, they also had to miss the birth of Ruth, their new cousin from Montana. But with restrictions now lifting, it was finally time to meet the baby.

With that first meeting on the horizon, the Bestmobile continued from Dickinson, North Dakota, across the border into Montana, past Billings, and through a

mountain range called the Bridgers. It was a beautiful area filled with vistas, tall pines and endless ranches that peppered the valleys. It looked like Texas and Alaska had a baby, which they called Montana.

Finally, they arrived in the booming city of Bozeman, a hip college town in the middle of the mountains. After driving all day, they were pleased to be approaching the house of their Aunt Carolyn and Uncle Kevin. They pulled into the driveway, gathered their backpacks and snagged their water bottles. Before they could approach the door, uncle Kevin came out onto the front porch and yelled out, "Welcome kids!"

They each gave their uncle Kevin a high five on the way in the door and were immediately met by an unexpected friend – their dog Phyllis. She is a golden retriever who is getting on in years – much calmer and wiser than a puppy. She was the kind of dog who can teach you something; not the other way around. It was the perfect situation for Hugo who was still just two years old – although he looked and acted like he was three.

As they climbed the steps into the living room, they found Aunt Carolyn sitting with baby Ruth, their young cousin.

"Hi kids! How are you?" Aunt Carolynn asked.

The kids were so happy to see their new baby cousin, that they completely forgot to answer their aunt's question, and ran straight over to see the baby.

"Hello Ruth!" Said Frederick.

"You're so cute, Ruth!" Said Edith.

"How are you, Ruth?" Asked Hugo.

Ruth looked at them all and giggled. She had a small tuft of dark hair, pretty brown eyes, and cute little ears. Their Aunt Carolyn explained that her middle name is Genevieve, so they can call her by her initials RG as a nickname. The kids loved it and called her that for the rest of the trip.

The next morning, after eating breakfast, Uncle Kevin went to work and Aunt Carolyn took the Best family to Bozeman Beach, which was at a delightful little lake situated between the Bridger Mountains on the outskirts of town.

They unpacked their beach gear, and helped Aunt Carolyn bring baby RG onto the sand. It was a wonderfully warm day to be at the beach. Who would've imagined they'd be having a beach day in Montana!?!

Frederick, Edith, and Hugo swam in the fresh mountain water and played in the sand. The lake was refreshing, but it wasn't just the lake that made them feel good; they felt good because they had finally connected with their new baby cousin. They had bridged the invisible gap that the pandemic had placed between them. In that valley in the Bridger mountains, two families were reunited at last.

HERDS AND TURDS

On the third day of the Best kids' stay in Montana, their Uncle Kevin offered to take them to the place where he works. Luckily, he doesn't work at a typical office or a factory, but for an organization called Eagle Mount, which provides outdoor adventures for people living with disabilities. At the Eagle Mount facility, Uncle Kevin had arranged for the kids to go horseback riding.

When they arrived, they noticed the scenic mountain range in the backdrop, and a wonderful facility that housed a swimming pool and a greenhouse – in addition to the horseback riding facility! But they also noticed something else – a real stinky smell!

"More poop!?!" Exclaimed Edith.

"Yep!" Said Uncle Kevin. "It comes with the territory."

As the kids stepped into the hay-filled arena, they met the horse trainers, and were each given a helmet. Frederick had a black one, Edith had a purple one and Hugo had a blue one. Then, the older two were both given a chance to ride around the arena, as the horses kicked a giant beachball. Hugo was too young to ride, but he ended up bonding with a miniature horse named Wizard by feeding him carrots.

After a fun day at Eagle Mount, the Best kids rested their heads one last time in Bozeman and bid farewell to baby RG. Before long, they were back on the road, and stopping to use the bathroom on the east

side of Montana. At one paricular rest stop, the kids noticed a funny sound in the grass. Every time they walked by, it sounded like rain falling to the ground. As they looked closer, they realized it was a swarm of grasshoppers hopping away whenever they came near! The kids got closer to witness this phenomenon, which was both intriguing and terrifying.

Crossing back into North Dakota, the Bests decided to stop one more time to see the Painted Canyon in the southern unit of Theodore Roosevelt National Park.

The sun was setting and their mom thought it would look extra beautiful in the evening. As they drove into the park, they first noticed purple and yellow wildflowers scattered all around them. Then, they spotted a massive herd of bison that was grazing in a field near the canyon. It was gorgeous!

When they reached the Painted Canyon area, they left the car and walked toward the canyon edge, but getting there wasn't easy. Why? Poop. Again. Yes, the kids had to navigate a field full of bison patties.

Thankfully, it was worth it, and their mom was right – the light of the evening sun was gleaming onto the Painted Canyon with shades of coral and orange. It was wild and wonderful, and everything they wanted the west to be.

FAR FROM PLAIN

North Dakota seems to get a bad rap. It's often the last state people visit, but the Best kids thought North Dakota was a hidden gem! In addition to being the home of Dot's Pretzels, North Dakota has a beautiful landscape, an incredible National Park, and some truly vibrant towns. It sits atop the great plains, and yet it's anything but plain.

As they traveled back from Montana, the Best kids got to explore a few extra places. On the eastern edge of Montana, they stopped to explore a dinosaur museum that had a t-rex breaking through the outside wall. Later, they drove into Bismarck, and sat on the grass outside the state capitol building. But their most exciting stop was in North Dakota's biggest city called Fargo.

As the team exited the highway and entered the downtown area of Fargo, Edith piped up and asked, "Where are we stopping!?"

"It's a surprise!" Replied their dad.

The truth was, the Best kids' mom and dad didn't know what would be open because of pandemic restrictions. Eventually, they came to a stop, and the kids' mom stepped into a building downtown. A few minutes later she returned and said, "We're good to go! It's open!"

They had arrived at the Plains Art Museum, which houses various galleries of traditional and contemporary art in a modern facility. The kids jumped out of the Bestmobile, put on their masks, and opened their minds as they entered the building.

The first thing they loved was
the air conditioning because
it was a really hot day in Fargo! The
second thing they appreciated was a clean bathroom
since they had been driving for quite some time.

Once they entered the galleries, they were pleasantly
surprised by the strange and wonderful art pieces on
display. They seemed to have a little bit of everything
– conceptual photography, abstract paintings, and
metallic sculptures made of mesh. The artwork wasn't
just interesting; it was relevant to the region and told
the story of indigenous cultures.

One notable series of little sculptures by Michael
Omundson featured three indigenous faces looking up
from the ground. They were made of resin
and painted black. Each one featured a
different animal headdress. They were
titled "Strength," "Connection,"
and "Wisdom."

Another series that stood out was from the featured artist in the main gallery named Dyani Whitehawk. Inspired by textile design, she presented an homage to Lakota women across 15 to 20 different pieces, each depicting strength and beauty with striking lines, colors, angles and statements.

For the Best kids, the experience was exhilarating. The artwork was visually exciting and the pieces on display sparked important conversations about colonialism, nature and displacement. The kids left the museum with some tattoos and stickers from the gift shop, but they walked away with something even greater – a new perspective on the state of North Dakota and a new understanding of its history.

LITTLE DETAILS

GRASSHOPPER SWARM

The swarm of grasshoppers the kids discovered at a rest stop in eastern Montana was mesmerizing. The region is filled with long, yellow, dry grass. Every time one of the kids took a step in the grass, they could hear the grasshoppers leaping, which sounded like rain on a rooftop.

HERB GARDEN

When the kids visited uncle Kevin's workplace, there was a quaint herb garden, which was maintained by the staff and the people they serve. The kids were offered samples of strawberries and mint leaves as they walked by the garden.

T-REX HEAD

In eastern Montana, the kids stopped at a creationist dinosaur museum. The many Bible references were a little heavy-handed, however, the giant t-rex head breaking through the exterior wall of the museum really drew the kids in!

FLOATING DOCK

At Bozeman Beach, where the kids swam with their cousin Ruth, there was a dock, but it wasn't for boats; it was for swimmers! This floating dock was perfect for climbing on top of, taking a rest on, and jumping off of in style!

BEST BITES

PURPLE GOOSE EATERY

In Barnesville, Minnesota, there's this wonderful, small town pub that does take out pizza. We grabbed one to go and took it to the pavillion at Blue Eagle Park in town to eat. Delicious!

EL RODEO

Our trip to Bozeman, Montana wouldn't have been the same without tacos made inside of an old school bus!

BEST BETS

THEODORE ROOSEVELT NATIONAL PARK,
DICKINSON, ND

Filled with wildlife and great views, this national park was definitely a highlight of the trip.

PLAINS ART MUSEUM
FARGO, ND

Experiencing art from the region we traveled to was wonderful; especially in the middle of a long journey home!

BLUE EAGLE PARK
BARNSVILLE, MN

This park was a peaceful spot for a picnic on a long stretch of driving. It had public restrooms and a huge hill to run down.

MUSINGER GARDENS
ST CLOUD, MN

On the drive home, these gardens were our playground! A stunning, rejuvenating place with fountains and flowers.

BOZEMAN BEACH
BOZEMAN, MT

The kids had a whale of a time swimming in the mountains with their baby cousin, Ruth.

RIVERSIDE PARK
MILES CITY, MT

This city park was a great size, and perfectly quiet. It had tall trees lining the road, a swimming pond, public restrooms and a nice playground.

BUMPS IN THE ROAD

TACO DOGS

One evening in Bozeman, the Best kids were walking with their cousin, and her golden retriever Phyllis to pick up tacos. They were sitting to eat at a public park when a vicious dog escaped from his leash and started attacking Phyllis. The kids' dad and Uncle Kevin tried to hold the dogs back from each other until the owner returned. It was a scary situation that left everyone a little bit shaken.

ZOOM CALL AT THE PARK

The Best kids' mom had just landed a new teaching job at a university, but her orientation meeting fell three days into their journey to Montana. Fortunately, she was able to join virtually through Zoom, while the kids had a picnic and explored Riverside Park in Miles City with their dad.

SNEAKY BISON

When the Best kids revisited Theodore Roosevelt National Park on the way home, they had to weave between piles of bison dung. The dung-weaving must have distracted them because once they got into their vehicle, they noticed a bison about 10 feet away. Luckily, they were already buckled up and safe inside.

LADY'S T-SHIRT

When the Best family went to the Plains Art Museum in Fargo, North Dakota, their dad purchased a black t-shirt as a souvenir. He was excited to wear it because it looked retro. Sadly, after getting home and trying on the shirt, he realized it was a ladies shirt, and was much too small for him.

OIL CHANGE

After driving through Michigan's Upper Peninsula, and into Wisconsin, the Bestmobile's check engine light appeared on the dashboard. This meant a stop at a local park in Wausau which was across the road from Fleet and Farm where Frederick and his dad took the car to get tuned up, while the others enjoyed the park.

ABOUT THE AUTHOR

The adventures of the Best kids found on these pages were chronicled by none other than their own father. Joshua Best is a writer, designer, and illustrator. By day, he leads the marketing team at a nonprofit network of children's hospitals. Of all these roles, there is none better than being a dad to Frederick, Edith and Hugo.

FOLLOW ALONG

Why wait until the next book is released when you can find out now where the kids are headed? Follow the kids on Instagram to watch illustration in progress and to see real photos of current trips! Also, check out the website for ways to get in touch, or listen to our podcast on Spotify, Google or Apple Podcasts.

@thebestkids_explore

@thebestkids_explore

thebestkidsexplore.com

The Best Kids Explore

www.ingramcontent.com/pod-product-compliance
Lightning Source LLC
Chambersburg PA
CBHW042055060526
44119CB00115B/293